Meanwhile

Meanwhile

Poems by Kathleen O'Toole

David Robert Books

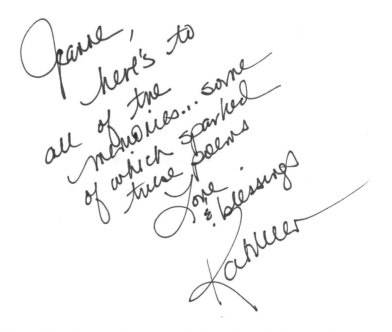

August 2012

Jeanne,
here's to
all of the
memories... some
of which sparked
these poems
Love.
& blessings
Kathleen

Published by David Robert Books
P.O. Box 541106
Cincinnati, OH 45254-1106

ISBN: 9781936370245
LCCN: 2010942894

Poetry Editor: Kevin Walzer
Business Editor: Lori Jareo

Visit us on the web at www.davidrobertbooks.com

Table of Contents

I.

II.

Acknowledgments

My thanks to the following publications
in which versions of these poems first appeared:

America: "The Magdalen, A Garden and This",
"Meanwhile"

Asphodel: "Awaiting My Aunt's Death I Take a Walk"

Beltway: "Demolition in a Time of Penitence"

Christian Century: "Statio"

Delaware Review: "Those Reels"

Little Patuxent Review: "Seen, Unseen"

Margie: "April Is", "Reading Obituaries"

Maryland Poetry Review: "Autumn DisSonnet"

Natural Bridge: "Portmuck Blackberries"

New Millennium Writings: "At Kelly Ingram Park"

Notre Dame Review: "Lives of the Saints"

Passager: "Small Comfort"

Poetry: "County Antrim Archeology"

Potomac Review: "Nothing but Gifts"

Prairie Schooner: "Salado Markings"

Runes: "Storm"

Texas Review: "Trust"

The Ledge: "Practice", "Real Presence"

White Pelican Review: "Caesura", "Sonoran Canyon"

A number of the poems in this book were included in *Practice,* a chapbook published in 2005 by Finishing Line Press.

Special thanks to the many circles of creativity in which I have been nurtured and supported: to John & Lena O'Toole, first and best teachers, to Nick Virgilio, Kadi Billman and Michael Doyle, who first named me *poet,* and to all the women of my longstanding Baltimore writers' group – Christine Higgins, Ann Lolordo & Madeleine Mysko, the longest standing.

For the time, and the natural and human ecosystems that have shaped many of these poems, I am grateful to Blue Mountain Center, The Bread Loaf Writers' Conference, Virginia Center for the Community Arts, and especially the Community of Writers at Squaw Valley....multo grazie!

Cover Art: photograph by Margaret Woodson Nea
Cover Design: Hilary Kay Doran
Author Photo: Christian D. Meade

Table of Contents

III

for John

I

Practice

We need in love to practice only this: letting each other go.
For holding on comes easily; we do not need to learn it.
Rainer Maria Rilke

It is the season of letting go.
Each tree strafed by November wind repeats the truth,
each leaf scraping pavement like a dog's paws.

Letting go of breath, of the sun's heat:
we feel it as we stand wind-whipped, in awe of geese that yield
calmly to the chill of the tidal pond where they feed.

When we embrace, the joy we feel is
urgent as if we possessed this moment alone.
Love lasts that practices the grasp

of marsh wrens leaping at reeds in wind,
the trust of a seagull's sudden uplift. Thus held
love may appear — or disappear — without warning

as migrating flocks ascend with the sound
of a low fire bursting into flame.

The Magdalen, A Garden and This

Strip all else away and we'd know only
that she was grateful, that she found her way
to the cross, and that she returned

to the tomb. A disciple for sure, not
Mary Sister of Lazarus, or the woman caught
in adultery or she who angered the men

by anointing Jesus with expensive oils.
This Mary of Magdala only named as one
from whom he cast out seven devils, followed

until that first day of the week, in the garden,
where, weeping at her loss, she was recognized,
became known in the tender invocation

of her name. *Mary:* breathed by one
whom she mistook for the gardener, he
who in an instant restored her—

gave her in two syllables a life beloved,
and gave me the only sure thing I'll believe
of heaven, that if it be, it will consist

in this: the one unmistakable
rendering of my name.

Portmuck Blackberries

It's easier here where hedges edge the lane
and the dark fruit shines openly
crowning old stone walls, easy to taste
the August ripeness one berry at a time.
Each morning and afternoon I sample
more of the last reds softened sweetly black
so that to taste is to remember
summer foraging, the pains we once took
to pick these berries, assembling in a
dutiful band — like altar servers — we
stood sweltering and overclothed but
protected from the woods in which we gathered.
We knew the ritual, the penance of thorns,
reaching for fingerfuls to fill the tins,
knew too our reward, to savor for days
that tart aroma of stewing, straining
the berries into jam, even while checking
our scalps for ticks, medicating the itch
of hands scored red from the dark thicket.
Now I collect no more than a handful,
select each berry to taste, and relish
the soft pulse of berry between thumb
and finger, where the sun plays black-silver
and sure against the skin of this new fruit.

The House, The Night of Lilacs

Once upstairs, I easily shed the borrowed skirt and
        tortoise-shell barrettes, like small sins
rehearsed from a catechism verse.   I could barely touch
        his skin there.
                                Afterwards
        he wanted to know why I had not — protected —
did I presume — and what was braver   — then ?

Early birdsong stealing from that novitiate
        the first Sunday of May   as Nixon sweated
toward resignation   I yielded   proudly
        rode my gentle friend,   almost maternally
as the great Cathedral bell tongued twelve.   It roused us
        rocked us   entwined with the shaking weight
of a freight train just beyond our reach

                                where this train
now passes.   The House is gone.   Removed, my secret
        monument   the pleasure each time I commuted past
as if spring rain   would forever fill the railway ditch.
                                        Today
        a flat, untended lot   leaves me to invent
a stone   a leaf   as marker. Would he
        even recall   Who   did (not) touch him
then?   Did we (either of us) leave
        a tender mark that still aches   —   a sigh
yet in the dust there   to   remember ?

Reading Obituaries

Suppose you had to supply the label
to summarize a life, choose the subtitle

to trail off with your name, an echo in printer's ink,
that inevitable last flash before you sink

into nameless oblivion: *governor's secretary, loved pets*
active in scouts. I've often wondered how apt the sobriquets

and who's to slap this inglorious footnote
upon you—from some unknown scrivener the quote:

collected stamps, invented polyester, wrote obituaries.
These days, with epitaphs passé and cemeteries

crowding corpses into drawers and under standard granite
tabs, what's to preserve you in words—a string of credit

reports, a toe tag at the morgue, and a column inch
or two, with picture if you've earned it, to cinch

your place. Like Jacob Besser, dead yesterday.
He alone flew on both the **Enola Gay**

and **Bock's Car**, Hiroshima and Nagasaki bound.
An engineer who—incidentally—found

and patented a pump to steady the heart in surgery,
exits dragging in pithy summary the legacy

he'd spent a half-life justifying. In these few words
his time-lapse afterimage: two mushroom clouds.

At Kelly Ingram Park

The wash of water over marble—a balm, like sweet gum
leaves shivering in the country. A few scattered clumps of locals
picnic or play checkers—where once water cannons —

Bronze sculptures placed at intervals on *Freedom Walk*
lead visitors past a jail cell with children's figures behind bars,
through Bull Connor's dogs, fangs bared and leaping—

while an ice cream truck's insistent calliope reprises
a Scott Joplin rag, and a Pepsi-logoed banner proclaims
the 132ⁿᵈ Anniversary of the Sixteenth Street Baptist Church.

Against the familiar brick façade, same lead-paned windows
and neon sign as in the grainy newsreels. I agree to photograph
some girls on the stairs   — where once the washroom—

I'm thinking how the un-oiled wheels of law just managed
to deliver a couple of 80-year old preachers, *former Klansmen*
in wheelchairs for their *life sentences*, of the composure

in Goodman's mother's voice, and who or what impulse to grief
brings me—whose grandmother lit candles in the dark fearing
the riots would spill our way in April of '68, whose parents

dressed her as Aunt Jemima for Halloween in '59—what
utterance can I tuck into some crevice of atonement ? Then
Vernon McCoy appears with a commentary in exchange

for bus fare, out, he says of Birmingham, where a Vietnam vet
can't get decent benefits—imagine in wartime— and how
he stood here in '63 at age fifteen (friend of the Collins sisters)

and that what you need to understand is this circle of black
marble, broken in four equal columns is for the murdered
girls and the water flowing from the broken place is tears.

Seen, Unseen

We do not fix our gaze on what is seen but on what is unseen.
2 Corinthans 4:18

First only the wings—a flash
         displacing mist above the pond at dawn.
A heron nearly tall as I, surveys the space before her:
         lily pad, darting insects, filtered light.   One tentative step, fluid
then wings pressing air, mist, silence.

Sierra ridge. We hike through a summer stand of aspen,
         delight in the shimmer and claque
of white-silver petioles in the breeze, when (we learn) it's
         14,000 stems, a one hundred acre ice-age miracle tree
articulating its one fervent desire.

Behold the moths—witless servants of the nearest filament,
         or moon migration specialists?
The green-head flies that light— and bite—
         can't have flown this far out onto the bay.
Nor the dragonfly poised on the halyard in a stiff nor'easter —
         as if it needs this fiberglass sloop to sail !

A change of heart. Imagine a movement
        among the super rich, rushing to cash in their billions.
A river of balm floods the sub-Sahara, overtakes
        the pillaging of AIDS. Only first *see* the mothers
queuing up at a Botswana clinic, their sons bending over cassava plots,
        sisters minding babies who play gamely in the dry stream bed.

———————————————

Or fireflies…lifting from the long grass
        at dusk…appearing as if from air
as if they were always there. Why not
        our dead, our ancestors, the heaven/hell around us
defying all we do not believe.

Losing Ground

How does one come to claim
the weight of place, these days,
I wonder, pocketing stories like stones
to mark each new river of migration.

A mother buried her infant's umbilical cord
in a garden: *No matter where you go,*
the land will always remember you.
Her son remembers, returns one day
to find in rich green rice fields
an island of tended graves,
a young farmer with an oxcart who explains:
they are ancestors;
they worked this land and now
their spirits will protect it.

The Doyles blessed their new home
taking live sods from the old hearth
in procession past the whin and whitethorn hedges
with the Sacred Heart.

When grandmother Domenica
butchered chickens in her garden
they scurried headless on the red ground
and each August the fig tree blushed its fruit
only for her careful winter wrapping.

This summer I buried a crow
in the yard, one who'd suffered noisily
in the yew all afternoon,
then I covered the spot
with pine boughs, Rose of Sharon.
I rent this place,
might move at any time.
The garden soil slips quickly through my hands.

Jardin, Morne Trois Pitons

Enter into a thousand variations of wet:
puddle, shower, pouring mist, drizzle curtain
through which the afternoon sun floods
the cabana. Fuguing rain.
                              One bead
on the elbow of an orchid stem – in it
the spectrum shimmers.

Chute d'eau. Uisge, gliding over gorges,
shaking free of winded fern and coconut palm,
scattering with it bird chant: squeal and chirrup,
worrel and caw.
                        Be still. Why
invent words for prayer ?

———————————————

Clouds above Dominica's
forested spine, bear daily rain.
We inhale   mist of streams
ascending   breath of giant tree ferns.
What's decaying returns through moss
and beetle, root worm and mold
to nourish banana palm and breadfruit blossom.
All other mothering—Antillean finch nestlings,
nursing mountain goats, my mother brushing,
brushing my hair—must proceed
from this: taproot, womb.

———————————————

Giant geranium and torch ginger,
          jade vine and heliconia
mask the steep footpath. Children
          name any green untamed place jungle,
not garden, air cleanser, shelter of bat,
          monarch butterfly, macaw.   Within
this rainforest we grasp   our own redundancy,
          encounter all that's wild: *tête chien*
or mangrove root uncoiling, serpentine
          as if to reel us toward the source—
our unclaimed darkness.

John 12:24 — Sierra Meditation

I.

How much energy is in a seed?
        don't expect the heroic   sprouting soprano solo

that seed— no more fecund than coal dust
        but for fragrant solar panels: Jeffrey Pine and juniper

hidden city of fungi spooning ooze
        from the underworld   into this inkling

II.

Unless the corn of wheat die
                    wrapping the fig tree

It is only a corn

        reaches   bog stillness   sinking

But if it die it brings forth   —

III.

Here's the thing:

        mountain pine beetle   tunneling in phloem

sacrificial loam   hot fire   then the burnt fingers

        dead —

release   fervent desire

        fall afresh

IV.

Butter wort and sneezeweed, bog laurel and Alpine goldenrod

Shaggy hawkweed, pink alum root, Anderson's thistle
                                      (Pray for Us)

Mule ears, mousetails, horsemint, stickseed and monkshood

Indian paintbrush, ranger's button, Whitney's locoweed
                                (Graciously Hear Us)

Sierra gentian, sierra onion, sierra shooting star

II

County Antrim Archeology

Two pounds approximately is what you'll be reduced to
after seventeen hundred years, others' atoms layered over
bones and bits of tooth, nail, and less and less you.
Two, four thousand years, twenty centuries of grief
have sanctified these grave stones. Land levels rise here,
as the sphagnum moss darkens, tightens, pressed to peat,
as tissue, tendons, heart meat blacken into a tangle
of root that will someday climb to cover sixteen feet
of round tower in its keep, claim the granite base
of a chapel, rosary beads, a bishop's gold crosier,
the soldier's gun, whatever weighs on this receptive
earth. Like a slow black hand, the centuries' tidal wave
crests to clear the coast of all rival claims to sovereignty,
until your own molecular mark sinks with the rest,
a small moist stain on the lip of the whirling god.

On Marrying over Fifty

Like swimming at 8,200 feet
the breath less sure, resistance—
weight of muscle and bone—recalibrates
sea level certainties.
                    The Hunter Moon
hovers, a stone on the footpath,
top half waxing down above a granite canyon
littered with sharp debris.
                        An extended arm
and its shadow.
                    We venture
ecstatic moths in lamplight—

into a centrifuge
landscape where fixed syllables
            si non
                    agus
                            ever
echo   the leap.

Those Reels

skip from Billy's accordion
skim the polished floorboards 'til
they land up under your heels

then swell into a pulse
that tips the scales of reticence
holding you fast.

Into a circle of arms
now twining, now reaching by,
the notes come skittering

alive in the glistening of flushed
faces, arched along flexed
calf muscles, legs

that spring against the gravity
of measured days. So out of place
in the city, these tunes

when they spill out
over the urgent bass
of sidewalk rap, above

the din of tin cans
and scrap in a pushcart, from the window
of a smoky bar—a stream

of flute, soft and absurd
as sheep would be, grazing in Bayview Park.
Yet there's more beneath

this breath. Under
the taut-stringed fiddle's a fire: grief
pressed to oil, to wine

to a dance
on the exile's grave.

Trust

As when the plane accelerates and lifts
us from the solid earth.
                      With the throbbing weight
of engine beneath my exit aisle seat, what else to do
but trust
             the invisible pilot
and the hands that riveted "hinge access panel"
to the wing, and the ones that oil and examine
the foreboding bowels of wire
                          between coffee breaks
and after arguments with lovers.   Someone in a tower
in Atlanta too, who may be nursing a migraine or planning
to leave his wife.
                  Trust in the indistinguishable
hydrogen that flaunts itself in cloud flocks suggesting
that again today
                gravity will not let me down.

I'll never convince you that God too
is in this lifting, this flight
                    and that I came to trust
as to healing:
            once I allowed that a surgeon
could saw and sew titanium into me, I could begin
the dance.
        Se confier, to have faith
with the currents that suspend this flight
as with your cottoned patch of shoulder as pillow
your offering of love
              unquestioned
as air.

Salado Markings

The Salado people were the best known descendents of the Hohokam.
They built hundreds of miles of irrigation canals along the Salt and Gila
Rivers. Casa Grande National Monument

I.
Lent begins. A lengthening dawn as pink light
      crests the Superstition peaks. Not much moisture here.
Still mute deer seek out hidden springs, and the jack rabbits
      and pocket gophers scamper between saguaro and paloverde,
prickly pear and mesquite, all prospecting the fast falling water table.

II
We migrants hoard the hope of spring in our bones,
      searching like divining rods for any thaw. Tohono O'Odham
         marked the new year at the ripening of saguaro fruit,
harvesting the buried seeds to grind on metate stones into flour.
      Juniper and piñón log, saguaro ribs fortify the mud
         of jacal ramada and vatro shelters still marking
the Sonoran desert with agile shade.

III.
Reverence echoes in the soft call of *okokokoi*—the white wing dove.
      A great horned owl hides in the towering shelter
over Casa Grande—until the park ranger discerns his cry.
      Hohokam venerated eagles, hawks and vultures, mountain sheep.
      Awls of cactus needles, whorls of potshards,
      censors and palettes of stone remain.
      Yet they left no bones for us to measure them.
Only the aligned portals through which the equinox sun rose and set,
      rose and set.

Opening: O'Keeffe Museum, Santa Fe

I will paint only black and white,
she said, *until I must have blue.*
Necessity arrived in waves
of sky and hills and violin shapes;
blooming.

Like a penitent after the long fast
the artist seasoned her palette
until each pastel wash of petal
deposits pink or plum
onto our tongues, cotton
candy—or Eucharist—melting.

Now communicants line up
to gaze into these floral pools
after an artist's reflection
all ego and flame.
                 But I want
to wander a while, inhabit an earlier
truth of spare black lines that bleed
into grey, the weight of swirls
in charcoal against shell, against bone.
In this clear desert light, if I am still,
I can enter the emptiness that dwells
in us, inhabiting in hers my own
wilderness.

Triptych

I. Silence

— the first thing you notice,
as if each is engrossed
in some inward utterance.

No way to pray this out.
Only finger each fragment:

> the sky, a maddening blue
> behind half-staffed flags,

> a lone piper flinging
> his wailing chords— *Amazing Grace*
> trails us into Union Station's arches;

> he, stock-still in his kilts, beneath
> the fifty flags of the states — a trembling

September breeze.

II. Word

Now their stories, voices, rain around us
In grey clouds of newsprint.

We know the quotidian they knew:
walk from the train, push
the *up* elevator button, remember
what you forgot.
Phone messages
were once normal.

Know too that they were
are   we   —
this consuming flame.

III.   Form

The potential of matter to hold
its opposite   to become
foreign: sand to glass,
vapor to ice, human and animal
lives to ash, and grass.

Now each overflight of a graceful winged thing
into fire.
                    Craters re-order geography,
architectural steel and mountains collapse
space into absence.
                    Sixteen acres
a sculpture not hewn, but incinerated
into icon.   When sunset disturbs the dust
or klieg lights oddly sanctify—
                                a Cathedral wall
its honeycombed embrace of air
and smoke, incenses
                    where the exoskeleton
rises, more hallowed each day
with what it surrenders
                    and what it cannot disclose.

Pentecost

after the painting "Ku" by Ken Krafchek

Tongues of fire
  tongue of shadow and ash
settling, unsettling—
  a crevice, just opening,
a caving in: mind
  and mindlessness, soul-singed
this time for good. Correspondence

descends
    as if from nowhere
window — or tomb;
  who will turn away
these graven stones ?

Breezy apparition:
    red-winged blackbird
red-tailed hawk, one carrying a new canto
  the other circling
carrion-eyed   circling.

Rushing wind
  from within
all light from depth
entered and entering
  still.

Theme and Variations: Baltimore Museum
Sculpture Garden

Tombstone granite chunks
                    perch at odd angles,
        sculpt the sun and shade of late July into a collage
with hasta blossoms and pin-oak saplings – explode
        the "Eight-Part Circle" into green
constellations.
            I weigh this idea
of disassembling the sum, hacking apart
its roundness   orchestrating anarchy—
        the chaos of a child's block play, of a will or whim
resisting order.
                    Heizer's pieces juggle
breeze   sunlight   the question
of separating   what you've wanted whole.

All smiles and seersucker-jumpered   a ghost
        breathes in this garden   in   out
walking her anguish away.
                    The last time
I summered slowly enough to linger here
        she peppered the leafy quiet with tales
of Tamoxifen, and lost ovaries, that remission
        she'd entered gracefully
                    not knowing
whether it would be her last.   In a speech this week
        a Senator painted a scene from her memory,
just the way my friend had once, hunting reasons:

small children playing in the fog
of DDT-spraying trucks, along tree-lined streets.
Ghosts of other summers
sacking promise.

Nuclear medicine, the technician explained
is only three steps of mind
— a few acrobatic sparks —
from the science of war.   I watch
the inscrutable screens moving dots
and what may be white
masses of organ or bone
as if my flesh were dissolving
shedding weight and substance.   Isotopes gallop
phosphorus charging   into this field.
The image—chaos to me—offers reference
only to the initiated   who *may* know
but *may not* interpret the cipher
the truth
my body holds.

Against summer harmonics of tree
            green   leaf curve   wind play   –   clash
angles and disfigurement of steel and stone:
John the Baptist stands skeletal and half-faced
            as if he heralded Hiroshima now too;
two resolute figures overtake him
            you'd imagine a mother and child
gone to market, but for the holes burning through
            decayed chicken flesh, gnawed
bodies, spirited from their rest.

So little consolation
                        until   here
delight   beneath a pillared silver twist   flying free
            as if a snip
of DNA helix had been carved out
            and exalted.   Merely stop   —   *it moves*
apprehending a fragment   of sky   or tree
            or cloud light   in its aluminum face.
Not quite an embrace.

———————————————————

Gratuitous blue   clouds heaped into the sky's catch
            of late-day sun, sliced by the pinging
syncopation of mast ropes lining the harbor. Imagine
            in a squint its dissolution   —   all of   it   —
light and sound
                        fractured into jigsaw-puzzle pieces.
Surgical.   Sudden as thunder.

                    Then say
the landscape re-assembles
                    someone throws you
a bow line, and an invitation to enter another
        life.   You are tempted
by the chance of sun   probability of storm
        guarantee of uncertainty
                    that could be your own
undoing.

One must still have chaos
        In oneself   (Nietzsche)
to be able to give birth
        to a dancing star.
        Chaos of question, chaos of desperation
                chaos breeding this
                    temptation to self destruct.
        Yet every day some dare
        to align themselves
knit a whole   improvised
        as artists scavenging street artifacts
for sculpture   selecting our own bits of chaos,
        reconnecting what was lost.
                    The new creation—
        a gathering of selves
                that dangle   exposed
        and salute each other   spinning on threads
of aspiration   attraction   never motionless
        dancing with death in our wings.

Proving Ground

June, and a silence embraces Fairlee Creek.
Silence woven of fish-splash and swallow chatter,
duck flight and the passive green of trees spilling
full syllables onto flat calm waters. Into this arena
rumbles the low-slung boat of a waterman,
thrusting its monotone grumble into surface ripples.
There's no hint of greeting in his face, fixed
as it is on the motorized line trailing
behind, trawling for crabs. He examines
each returning chunk of bait, ready to lunge
net in hand at any hint of motion. Along
the length of this once bountiful inlet, he'll pull
only a handful now in a morning haul.
                                                    Across the bay
another work is underway, its target indecipherable,
no motion in it like the heft of the catch.
But the locals know, someone's back at work
on another river, invisible behind the tree line,
behind the thundering of shells, which marks
the days here, regular as a great ship's clock.
They're testing the instruments of the next war,
carefully calibrating trajectory and firepower,
sampling ammunition and explosives. No way
to distinguish the face of those trawlers, or divine
the terminus of their work's trailing line.

Storm

Afternoon of March winds –
        surprise cloudbursts drench the fat squirrels
in my yard.   Sunshine, blowback,
rainbows, disheveled branches:
        litter of a year of war.
 How arrogance has strewn the landscape
                with shrapnel, voices and limbs
that recriminate.   *Coalition provisional*
                no authority here— or safety in words
like *enduring freedom.*   Chastening thunderbolt
and I wonder why we are spared.
                        On the corner
rows of Buddhist peace flags
                raveling with each new storm.

April is National Poetry Month

The cab driver's from Sierra Leone.
He recoils at the lawyer's voice on the radio
defending the serial arsonist: "My client
only set these fires to relieve stress!" We both
rue the absurdity, the chasm between words
and sober realities, his corner of the world
abandoned by Cold War interests, leaving
the vultures of chaos free reign with home-grown
(Harvard educated) rebels swooping in
while the one remaining superpower
has its back turned. Springtime in Washington.
Dependable as the cherry blossoms, white
dogwood in bloom, the latest fashion in barricades.
A bagpipe busker in a stand of azalea
plants a blush on the Capitol's marble cheek;
grackles forage in the mulch around a bed
of purple pansy. Red, white and blue tulips,
a cab driver from Sierra Leone. Poetry
is where you find it.

Nothing but Gifts

There are nothing but gifts on this poor, poor earth.   Czeslaw Milosz

Let us have a blessing for the dust
that coats our clothing, and our lungs
into which it migrates in clouds from dry
road beds, the dust kicked up by the tires
of matatus and safari vans, and from under the feet
of Kenyan women and men walking the shambas.
Let us have a blessing for the dust.

Let us have a blessing for the glass
shattered, arranged in shards to crown the high stone
walls that divide the rich from the poor,
church compounds from shanties and slums,
offices of the government and NGOs from blocks
of apartments for servants and transport workers.
Let us have a blessing for the glass.

Let us have a blessing for the smoke
that emanates from charcoal fires for cooking
goat stew and boiling water for bathing, pungent
smoke from industrial stacks and from piles of trash
smoldering at the outskirts of villages, smoke
of cook fires in Maasai huts in the evening.
Let us have a blessing for the smoke.

Let us have a blessing for manure,
from modest leavings of sheep and goats on the path
to the cow dung that carpets the villages of the Mara
and the large dried piles of it, laced with straw
that signal the passage of elephants in the bush,
the farmers' gold turning hillsides green with maize.
Let us have a blessing for manure.

Let us bless small mounds of green, thousands
of them dotting the savannah, where new life
sprouts from the decayed carcasses of zebra,
gazelle and wildebeest once given as food
to the predator, and now after dirt and blown
seed have mingled to yield grass or greenheart.
Let us bless the flowering of the mounds.

Let us bless the equatorial sun, in its fiery tango
at sunset, also the roots and leaves and scrub
that it coaxes up to feed the warthog and the village,
the rain when it comes and the wisdom of the elders
who whittle acacia into walking sticks and spears,
raise cattle and many children still blessing the land.
Let us bless the harsh and bountiful sun.

Statio

For once, silence—
genuine calm. Forty minutes
on a tidal bight with a great blue
heron   in the binoculars'
          sight.
                    Not frozen
but still.
          In a half hour, she barely turns
a full 360 degrees.
                    Time to notice
the dark wingtip markings,
light not-blue-but-gray breast feathers,
the cobalt dash between the long beak
and dark-eyed crown.
                    Expectation
gives way to awe, as each degree
thins her to a reed among reeds.

By sunset, barely an apostrophe
against the green marsh
                    what's left of color
bleeds into water,
into this resolve:
                    to pause
to practice, to attend.

Winter of Ice and Straw

1.

So little evergreen, in these hills
so few bursts of pine fir to break
the mute browns of mud and bark, grass straw
yellow, and the weathered grey of shed
and barn, fences.
                              Morning illumination:
a quarter-mile stretch of barbed-wire, molded
overnight into a line of icicles around so many fists
of rust. Backlit with sunrise, such clarity
sculpts a tension of opposites, reprises
a tribulation in these Virginia mountains;
sunshine shredding itself
on the hundred tiny spikes of thorn bush
branching back skyward.

2.

In a cemetery in Tubberpatrick, Ireland a century-old oak
wears the prayers of the countryside—strips of rag tied
onto the long-dead native hardwood. Worn from memory
now, the name of the saint who's said to have hallowed
the tree, even the healings granted. But it's known all
around that the ground consecrates the remains of their
hanged heroes, and how the local farmers dragged the
bodies to midnight burial, matted with straw and blood,
fields away from the barn where their cornered lives were
ground out.

3.

At nightfall here
      it's the 'black ice'
on the roads that kills.
      Frozen patches of invisible script
signing curves and hollows with epitaphs—
      illegible until they're interpreted
by speeding tires
             already
out of control.

4.

The crossings are iced up the highway where a young mother figures her chances. A wager she's making this winter, not fully knowing the road. Nights for studies and dreaming awake while the boys slumber. Beat the clock, armed with as much schoolwork as she can cram between shifts, the rides to fetch children, the weary hours. It's a schedule etched in her bones (not hers alone) told to spin straw into independence, up that mountain slope. Quick, before the slow thaw drives hundreds like her into the one lane cleared for passage.

5.

Which birds are scavenging
the underbrush and hedges and what
do they require to survive
                                        until spring?
Watch the dipping flight of bright cardinal
pairs dodging each other for boxwood
cover. A clatter of blue jays tap at iced maples
as if gauging sap flow. Just how much
bounty is burrowed in a landscape
so thoroughly stripped
            that the wind's shrill note
etches only blackbirds dipping toward night
            plaintive as a scarecrow's shadow ?

6.

Today's full color photo above the fold: an Afghan family
making bread of grass, their final hedge against famine.
Grinding dried grass in winter on the stone face of war—
salt water for binding what remains into a crust. What tree
could elevate such strands of prayer to Mecca? Raw hands,
hollow eyes. Silence willing straw to flour. Head scarves
lift with the snow-edged mountain winds.

III

III

Meanwhile

A photocopy of my mother's heart,
neatly folded, falls from the leaf end
of *Yeats' Collected.*

Her cardiologist has drawn squiggles
and blobs to mark the arteries
blocked: *diffuse 80%, 70% plaque,*

more squiggles for the bypasses
the heart has patiently grown
to feed its urgent muscle.

Eggshells. Nitroglycerine.
The muffled tick
of a ship's clock on the mantle.

Each of us will have a turn
at this watch, with or without
warning. Meanwhile

I'm folding away neat piles:
the scolding that most stung,
butterscotch icing licked from the bowl,

a hairbrush (knick-knack, plate of pasta)
thrown in anger — the Silence after.
The trunk will be scented: gardenia,

garlic, Chanel No. 5. Meanwhile,
I collect figs from the garden, whisper
a decade of the Rosary, a Psalm—

the lake at dawn
a red-winged blackbird
rustles the reeds.

The Luminous World

Beside the candle flames this Advent Sunday,
a blind cantor sings of brightness in the coming
of the Lord. I find that year to year I hoard
more illumination to store for sunless days,
recording gradations of luster and shadow
calibrating brilliance.
                        What value etches
in memory remains: a September seawall,
chill-filtered light rinsing waves to opaque green
beneath radiant brush strokes of breakers; or
that winter solstice leaving Brussels near dusk—slow
motion sunset before us, the dark diagonal of night
behind, suspending a crescent moon with Venus
rising; until our final forward thrust spilled us
into crimson over Manhattan's frozen skyline.

Tonight the fervor in a sightless poet's voice
painting bright stones of desire, leaves me to wonder
where I'd find grace, without the luminous world.

Real Presence

I brought communion amid the quickening
of blossoms announcing: pink, dogwood, alive,
and at that hospital door began clutching
time, measuring my awareness constantly.

Now the loss that penetrates August,
when hours of light seem to be sliced
from both ends of the loaf, consumes me.
The nights, draped with cricket and locust

are thickening and thinning all at once.
From here, I'm not surprised to feel mortality
like the facial bones of the dying, protruding
more each day, until the skin seems indecent cover.

So I continue to gather pear petals, to hold
the white wafer we shared against a single day's
distraction, hoping I won't miss my last breath
of grape iris, or the last ripe fig before fall.

Labyrinth Walk

Outside the monastery, the August air is empty
but for bird psalm as the schola gathers to ground
our walk: plainchant at dawn. Planted by a pine
tree's face, I invoke beloved names at the touch
of each tight-fisted green cone and find the flower
of brown spent ones on the same tree. Shadow

and sun play at the entry to the path. My shadow
leads me in. Black-eyed susans laced onto empty
day-lily stalks. The rounded center of the flower
echoes the pine cone empty of seed. Stubbly ground—
each barefoot step awakens presence. At the touch
of sun-warmth on shoulder, I ponder a pine

cone's hydraulics. It soaks in moisture, pines
to shed all that's inside, until its shadowed
ridges invite the light in. I bend to touch
myself in purple clover. *Forgive what's empty.*
Words well up and flash with tears to ground.
Walk within the shadow. Make this wild flower

your core. I raise a handful of nearly flower-
ing clover— white-crowned echoes of pine
knots holding pollen—beseech the ground
for release. A sun break delivers the shadows
of other penitents into my path as the empty
center nears. Finally the impulse to touch

another in silence. The woman turns to touch
my breast where once a hematoma flowered
for weeks. Her own about to be emptied
of malignancy. A large seedless pine
cone tilts at a sunflower crown's shadow.
Dead center of the wheel. Knees to ground

me in this consciousness. This sacred ground
weaving in whorls beckons me to touch
each chakra, turn the empty womb's shadow
inside out to birth a hallelujah flower
without seed. So enfold the pollen silently, pine
beetle of prayer, hand it to the wind empty.

Return incensing this ground: from golden flower
and centering touch until the dancing soul pines
for its lost shadow. Seedless. Fruitful. Empty.

Autumn DisSonnet

I didn't want the fall to come this year,
clung like never before to each hour
of daylight, the deceptive comfort of sun
in thinning air. I wrapped myself within
a leafy shawl, fine as the Emperor's cloak.
I had forgotten that emptiness is home.
Now sharp stars carve their truth brilliant
in the first early darkfall, a new chilling
wind sweeps illusion away, leaves
the branch stripped of every grief :
the frayed chords of Delta Blues, that letter,
gone. His words disintegrate like smoke,
or wisps of an airplane's midnight wake;
dry leaves, they stir in the wind and scatter.

Yeats Catching: for my Father

Tread softly, because you tread on my dreams. WB Yeats

mornings
you almost always were
the first up

make 'em pitch to you !
good eye !
choke up on the bat
follow through

ours was the house with the bases
worn into the back yard grass
you the permanent pitcher
coaching all the neighbor kids

' *Pitch is wide !*
The Ump is blind !
you turn your head, adjust
the volume, ask me
to repeat myself.

I thought you'd left me
that I'd caught you stealing
third. Or tagged you
out before you touched home.

But yesterday I felt you in me.
as I crouched behind
the plate, in the stance
you drilled into us—
the ferocious will
in my swing.

Sonoran Canyon

There's something about the desert, beneath
this stretched canopy of cloudless sky,
the first cleansing breath of aromatic dry
heat, penetrating as ether—that can release
you onto an interior sea. Discover the crescendo
of your heartbeat, with the ever ascending tick
of time in the marrow of your bones,
feel the calluses of old scars like stones
in sand, like pits at the center of ripe fruit.

Here the wind swish of canyon lake laps at grassy
stubble like a cat's tongue, rhythmic and rough,
grooming. These days, I relish the jagged cut
rim of a sandblasted valley. As I age, I fancy
more arid beauty: these scrub-tufted
outcroppings of rock, a ruddy mesa lifted
above the desert floor. Perhaps in such dearth
of cover astonishment returns, to know earth
barren as Sarah, yet cradle dreams, expectancy.

Demolition in a Time of Penitence

Is this not the kind of fasting I have chosen: to loose the chains of injustice
and untie the chords of the yoke..? – Ash Wednesday, Isaiah 58: 6

For weeks the demolition experts have been at work—
picking clean the carcasses of four public housing high-rises.
They've stripped away the remains of family dwellings

right before our eyes: grease stains on mauve paint
and mad-flowered wallpaper, then the walls, wiring and pipes—
all the metal veins that pumped and plumbed lives.

For a moment our skeletons are out of the closet,
the underbelly of public will exposed. Some spring
Saturday, crowds will gather as if for fireworks

or a hanging. They'll applaud the timed sequence
of rubble-rending blasts. Yet, in that explosion memory
fragments will charge the air: salt taste of summer nights,

a mother's eyelids closing for the last time, the footsteps
of the late-for-dinner child, a fist print on the door.
Left dangling in the silence, with dust—the questions.

Small Comfort

God will settle this on judgment day.
Thomas Blanton, Jr., convicted May 2001

How will we settle such a score, heal a scar
still leaking toxins like those train cars
in an old tunnel under Baltimore?
Thirty-eight years, and still the pure

terror of that September day in Birmingham
returns in voices that flutter and land
like acid rain on my skin. Penetrate and
alarm us. Sarah, sister of Addie Mae, hand

us the mirror, the shards of glass you carried,
your lost eye. You become us, become me
holding evidence of what was unleashed
in my name and seeping still under harried

streets we tread. How to read the convicted
bomber's face, his jaw set, depicted
for us—as us—ascribing justice to his white
God ? I have seen this face of hate

under bowler hats in Ulster; but my rage
to sentence him—even multiplied by four—
won't incinerate all complicity that courses
still in *we.*   Turn the page:

uncertain future,   *rumblings of protest,*
little comfort.   Sarah— *someone ought to be* — left
to see   with our one clear eye.   Still
we   possibly   shall.   (Will we?)

Caesura

A late summer sun teases the bay
beneath the ferry making port, silent as thought.
In memory I am on that boat, in mid-November.

The years since are layered like the wool bundling me
when I glimpsed you alone on the dock.
Perhaps you could not see me

and I did not rush to the bow to wave
except in my heart. Yet I felt the space between us
collapse to inches between extended hands.

Still today we dwell in the held breath
between proposition and response. The laughter
of that evening, and a salt marsh sky filled with stars

float to the surface now and then—
in the unintended spark of a glance, an awkward pause—
and leave behind like driftwood

the unspoken question of what might have been
or yet be waiting: a ferry in the mist
unboarded.

Counting the Sorrowful

(1)
Mystery: in the last quarter hour
before dawn, the birdsong crescendos
as if heralding the light. Does this aural
palpitation—earth-beat—translate a
yearning? Perhaps we simply hear
more clearly in the absence of sight.

(2)
A walk in the damp chill of late
October: memories swept into a carpet
of pine needles gone to dust.
Overhead, waves of geese bark in rounds
as each flèche ascends, platoon-like on cue.
What signal or relation triggers their flight?
Regrets too, sure as the harpist's fingers
scaling each taut string.

(3)
I want them to sing lots of songs
at my funeral, my mother whispers
in the middle of a wedding, a wedding ex-
haling glitter and careful touches, heartache
stitched into the silence between toasts,
into the too-sharp Ave Maria notes.
But you're tone deaf, I'm thinking, all
the while transposing her words, pressing
lavender into the folds of her voice
so I won't forget.

(4)
After the chaos wrought by a few drops
of blood on his retina, my lover stirs: *in
my dream... my dad's laughter...he'd have loved
the surgeon's quip: this laser fix as spot
welding.* I'm adjusting his black eye patch
and picturing just how my red skirt
was hiked for the class photo, amazed
at the anarchic logic of memory.

(5)
In fifth grade, all the sorrowful mysteries
were broadcast from the small brown box
mounted high on the front classroom wall.
The principal's voice lost its stern rasp
only when inviting special prayer: first
my uncle's sudden death— his young family...
And again that November Friday, before the gray
flashes of a nation's mourning would paralyze us
for days, the whole school prayed the Rosary
led by the voice from the box, grief
accumulating with each decade.

Lives of the Saints

We children chimed in as the touchstone
names rang out—*Agatha and Lucy,*
Agnes and Cecilia, Perpetua and Felicity—
hypnotized by the timbre if not yet
the tales of these women—*all ye holy virgins*
and martyrs. A tide of syllables like algae
in opaque waves of faith—breakers
shaping the shore.
                         Only now the urge
to forge new icons. Felicity the maidservant
in sunflower cloth, quiet grace of the Ogoni
woman navigating crowded roadsides
balancing a giant yam in a basket on her head.
The arc of fabric from her raised arm
swaddles her belly. Just a hint of the child to be
softens her stride, the blaze of her eyes.
Perpetua in jade robes and Igbo head cloth
takes her seat in the dusty shadows
to nurse the son born in captivity, brought
to her daily, against her father's will.
A shaft of light from a single window
illuminates the heavy folds of cloth, smooth
skin of a noblewoman's hands, her steady
gaze and brazen hosannas.
                        One last image
framed in the instant the names *Perpetua*
and Felicity are joined, before a wild cow and
jeering crowds we do not see. Just two women,
arms entwined as if lifting to us
their truth: in love a leveling.

We do not name their companions. The story
once rivaled the gospels as Christian currency—
their courage, their kiss before death,
the white robes radiant, bloodless.

Baltimore, 1993

The first issue is always recognition.   Saul D. Alinsky

The police commander shuffles his papers
never looking up, never looking into
the faces that look at him, who see
behind his aversion a trail of ancestors,
of authority's faces, always averted
when white sheets bled the night,
diverted as justice suited itself. Don't look
to these eyes to recognize your face
distant son of Ashanti, daughter of X.
The mirrored shades are in his head,
reflecting only the blind and empty light.

A break in the action. Down the rain-cleared
street, I enter a McDonald's, still on edge.
Beside me a man drags a worn duffle: all
his belongings, I guess, along with the clothes
on his back. He dumps his pockets out
onto the counter. Three packs of matches,
four quarters, some loose small change. *Coffee,*
he mutters. The youths behind the counter
exchange grins. Their eyes say it all.
His never look up, never look out
from the footage that must be reeling inside.

Before this night ends, I'll agitate the leaders
who noticed the commander's grunts and nods,
name the power gained with signed agreements
on official paper, even see recognition dawn
in a few faces. I know my dollar's worth of burger
won't begin to remedy the bag man's hunger,
yet that moment turned the youngsters' gaze
his way. On these streets epiphanies are dear.
Cost and consequence blur once I arrive
home to unbend my own face in the mirror.

Legacies

I.

The whisper of baptismal waters' spray
has sealed this fate: mine the role of joining.
Carried to the church three years to the day
past grandfather Dominick's death, this keening
month would stretch ten years to heft his wife
Domenica's silver coffin up those same stone
stairs. First death's relics: my aunt's knife-
edged "Mom why did you leave me?" alone
at the open casket; my mother weeping in the dark;
all of them thinking me too young at ten to march
with my cousins. So I pressed the scene,
a cold coin against some molding clay within,
firm today as Nettie's hand that wouldn't loosen
from my shoulder, my grip on the high oak pews.

II.

Cleaning the attic, I stare at the smudged face
of my bride doll, two shapely feet in lace
and plastic, now sticky from thirty years of exile—
veil gone, net bodice crumpled against her still
perfect breasts, eyes blue as on my First Communion.
In photos, I clutched her white against my own.
The afterimage streaks into dreams like a bonfire
through scrapbooks of holy cards and movie star
smiles, as mine were practiced for grade school beaus,
flashed in pastel for proms. As they decompose
the lies leave traces, marked currency in the stream
of consciousness, still tossing out crimson
ribbons that laugh back across the pages
staining play programs and dried flower bouquets.

III.

Against a Gothic column of stone, Saint Patrick
is huddled in effigy. He seems to cower in his niche
beneath the towering spires. Beside my father, I remember
the low curve of Galway hills, far from these somber
arches thrown at the sky, wrought iron scrolling
into grates and gates as if to contain the holy.
Restraint of joy—like great-grandmother Nora's face—
this granite pressing a vein of bitterness into place,
mortar sealing the disappointment, stacking weight
against the escape of angry words, the self hate
that runs so deep in these kin. Hammer on anvil,
the priest's voice strikes no flint. My father's candle
flickers in a doused row. A few March rays infiltrate
the rosettes with a sudden shower of light.

Blazing, The Heat

I am the prickly green cone, thrusting its angled chambers out
   puckered yet guarding my seed.
My spit sizzles on the winding pavement: *no through street.*
First sight of a robin's headless remains—the *s-s-s-s*warming flies.

What color is my heat? Lime green like the wolf lichen
   nesting on a chunk of glacial till.
Thrilling cobalt of a Stellars Jay, pigmentless scales tricking the sky.
Imaginary bagpipes tilting up the slats of lodge pole pine. Watery light.

Three days to find the cutting board in its hiding place.
Three days to notice the vase of mountain heather on the bookshelf,
   the kind that winds me in its sorrow.

White butterflies pollinating the lavender—as if we weren't at war,
   as if the dust of innocents were not lining our sandals.
Bones too in the terminal moraine behind the 7-11, where a glacier
   dragged its detritus to rest.

Spin out — in creation descended from chaos, trailing its birthmark.

Awaiting my Aunt's Death, I Take a Walk

In the breeze-whipped center of a pond
a white heron appears as if risen from dream,
and moves slowly forward, stretching its full-lit feathers
bright against pond-green, tree-green shadows.

A motion in the shallows draws my eyes
until I see the partner—a great blue
indistinct as mist—first beckoning, then leaning in,
becoming the dancer's mirror in its sway.

For a moment the graceful birds face off—
a canoe's length of still water, air and sunlight
between; all motion, sound suspended for a breath.

Then gray-blue wings arch out, smoke against sky.
Soul dance, death sting: fly.

Notes

1.   "Jardin, Morne Trois Pitons" (page 24)
In its history the Caribbean island Dominica has been under English and French control. While now part of the British Commonwealth, the patois is French influenced and many of the place names remain French. *Morne Trois Pitons* is the National Park that covers most of the mountainous rain forest. "Tête chien" is the familiar name for a boa constrictor native to the region.

2.   "Pentecost"   (page 41)
"Ku" is one of a series of abstract paintings which developed out of Ken Krafchek's Buddhist practice, which he has exhibited with an invited "dialogue" – poetry and prose reflections of colleagues from the Maryland Institute College of Art and others, inspired by his work.

3.   "Theme and Variations: Baltimore Museum Sculpture Garden" (page 42)
The artists whose sculptures – part of the permanent collection at the Baltimore Museum of Art, Sculpture garden – referenced in this poem are:
Michael Heizer   " The Eight Part Circle"
Germaine Richier   "Tauramachy"
Jose Ruis de Rivera   " Construction 140".

4.   "Statio"   (page 51)
One of the elements of Benedictine spiritual discipline, the practice of pausing between activities to become conscious of the moment, of the presence of God.

5.   "Winter of Ice and Straw" (page 52)

Many of the rebellions of Irish Catholics against the British in 1798 ("The Year of the French") are legend in the countryside where they are commemorated by detailed markers in cemeteries such as this one in County Longford.

About the Author

Kathleen O'Toole has combined a more than thirty-year professional life in community organizing with teaching and writing. Her creativity was nurtured in a family of actors in Wilmington Delaware, where her parents founded and ran a dinner-theater, and her mother introduced young people to theater. In 1991 she received an MA from Johns Hopkins University, and has taught writing at Hopkins and at the Maryland Institute College of Art. She currently works for V.O.I.C.E., an affiliate of the Industrial Areas Foundation in Northern Virginia, and lives in Takoma Park, Maryland, with her husband John Ruthrauff.

CPSIA information can be obtained at www.ICGtesting.com
Printed in the USA
BVOW042136101111

275832BV00001B/39/P